AN
INTERPRETATION
OF ISLAM

An Interpretation of Islam
By Laura Veccia Vaglieri

Copyright 1957

By the Ahmadiyya Movement in Islam, Inc.

© **Islam International Publications Ltd.**

Published by:
Ahmadiyya Muslim Association UK - The London Mosque
16 Gressenhall Road, London, SW18 5QL

First edition: Printed in USA in 1957 by McGregor & Werner, Inc, Washington, D.C..

Second edition: Printed in UK in 2002 by Raqeem Press, Tilford, Surrey.

Third edition: Printed in UK in 2012 by Raqeem Press, Tilford, Surrey.

ISBN: 978-0-85525-996-9

Cover design by: Yusuf Ginai

An Interpretation of
ISLAM

by

Laura Veccia Vaglieri

Translated from Italian by:

Dr. Aldo Caselli, Haverford College, Pennsylvania

With a Foreword by:

Sir Muhammad Zafrulla Khan
Judge, International Court of Justice

THE AMERICAN FAZL MOSQUE
Washington 8, D. C.

PUBLISHERS' NOTE

The publishers are happy to acknowledge the indebtedness which they and the students of Islam owe to Dr. Laura Veccia Vaglieri, Professor of Arabic and History of Muslim Civilization at the University of Naples, Italy, far writing such a concise and objective study of the faith of Islam.

We are equally indebted to Dr. Aldo Caselli who took upon himself the arduous and difficult task of translating this book from Italian. Dr. Caselli received his Ph. D. from the School of Economics of the University of Naples. He spent several years in the Middle East widely travelling and studying the Arab people. Many of his articles on Islamic culture and institutions have appeared in the Italian press. Dr. Caselli arrived in the United States in 1938. At present he is on the staff of Haverford College, Haverford, Pennsylvania. It is a pleasure to have the first English translation of this important work done by such an eminently qualified scholar.

Our thanks are also due to Sir Muhammad Zafrulla Khan, Judge of the International Court of Justice, for writing a very valuable Foreword for the English edition of this work.

This book was originally published under the title of *Apologia dell' Islamismo* by A. F. Formiggini, Rome, Italy, in 1925.

KHALIL AHMAD NASIR

The American Fazl Mosque
Washington 8, D.C.

Contents

Foreword

The close of the sixth and the opening of the seventh century of the Christian era was, perhaps, the darkest period of the Dark Ages. Religion, morals, culture, philosophy and learning were all at a low ebb. Only a flicker, here and there, seemed to emphasize the universal gloom.

Over the Arabian Peninsula, the darkness was at its deepest. The absence of any form of organized government left life and property insecure, except insofar as family and tribal pacts and feuds might afford respite or maintain a rough balance. The dwellers of the peninsula were ignorant alike of the arts of peace and the rules of war. Rapine and brutality were the order of the day, restrained only by notions of a rude chivalry and hospitality and the urge of self-preservation against retributive action by those who could muster a superior force.

Neither seer nor philosopher could have opined that healing and salvation would come out of Arabia.

Yet that is what came to pass. A solitary voice was, under Divine Command, raised in Mecca, calling men to the worship of One God and proclaiming that through responding to this call would mankind achieve true dignity, honour, prosperity and happiness both here and hereafter. That voice was the voice of Muhammad, the Prophet of Islam.

That voice was truly a voice in the wilderness. It was received with laughter, scorn and ridicule. Only here and there one lowly and humble of heart responded with a courageous "Aye". As slowly, very slowly, "Aye" began to be added to "Aye", the laughter and ridicule changed into persecution; bitter, cruel, savage and sustained. The sole reason for this savage and prolonged persecution was the affirmation of faith in and the worship of One God on the part of the Muslims.

If faith in God was to be preserved and fostered, escape from Mecca was the only way. Some left, but were followed and their return was demanded from the sovereign of the territory across the narrow sea who had given them shelter. After hearing both sides he rejected the demand.

Thirteen years after his ministry had commenced, Muhammad himself received the Divine Command to leave Mecca. He slipped out in the company of a single faithful follower, Abu Bakr, at a time when his house was surrounded by a band of his enemies who had resolved to put a violent end to him that night. When his flight was discovered, the Quraysh of Mecca organized a pursuit but failed to discover the place where he had hidden himself along with his companion. The Quraysh then proclaimed a reward of one hundred camels for anyone who would produce Muhammad before them, dead or alive.

Eventually the Prophet and Abu Bakr made their way to Medina. Here the Prophet was not only joyfully received by the small party of Muslims, but was, by agreement between the different sections of the people of Medina, invited to take on, in addition to his functions as Prophet, the duties and responsibilities of chief executive of Medina. He thus became also the Head of a State. On learning this the Quraysh, who had already set a price upon his head, began to organize the Arab tribes in a series of alliances designed to bring about his destruction and that of his companions and of those who might dare to lend him their aid or support. A state of war was thus ushered in, in pursuit of a relentless purpose.

To the Prophet's many and various responsibilities and anxieties was now added the responsibility for the defence of Medina and the protection of the increasing number of Muslims scattered in all parts of the peninsula. He, on his part, also proceeded to win the good will of the tribes and to make treaties with such of them as could be persuaded to make common cause with him in the promotion of law and order and the maintenance of peace. The foundations were thus laid of the *pax Islamica*.

In the new roles thus imposed upon the Prophet, he acquitted himself with the highest credit. He proved himself a wise leader, a farsighted statesman and a courageous but humane and merciful commander. He and his followers had to contend against heavy odds and had to endure severe privations and sufferings, but the first stage of the struggle, which at the start had appeared utterly hopeless, was carried to a triumphant consummation when Mecca, without any bloodshed, opened its gates to the erstwhile fugitive and his companions within eight years of his flight therefrom. Then was witnessed the spectacle of the most magnanimous and generous act of forgiveness of which history furnishes a record.

We thus observe that not only Islam lays down correct principles for the beneficent regulation of all aspects of human relations and conduct, the Prophet of Islam was, through the Divine Mercy, also vouchsafed the opportunity to illustrate in his own life their successful application. Islam permits the taking up of arms only in defence and expressly forbids aggression. The Quran designates war as a conflagration which must be put out as speedily as possible, as often as it breaks out. Islam condemns and forbids all brutal and savage practices and customs of war and has instituted a set of rules designed to render even war humane.

9

The Muslims received divine permission to take up arms in defence of freedom of conscience and to establish peace and order. Their success against overwhelming odds aroused jealousy and apprehension, first among the Arab tribes and later on the part of the Byzantine and Iranian empires. These two great Powers could not reconcile themselves to the sudden emergence of the united, progressive and dynamic republic of Islam. It constituted a challenge to all the values upheld by these two empires. Islam made a strong appeal to the oppressed and exploited peoples that were subject to their authority. The inevitable followed. A conflict ensued which opened the way for the spread of Islam to the confines of the then known world.

Within an astonishingly brief period, over vast areas darkness and confusion were dispelled, order was established, all manner of beneficent institutions sprang into life, a high moral order was set up and the blessings of knowledge, learning and science began to be widely diffused. The world experienced an astounding revolution. This was no freak spectacle; no sudden flare up followed by an even more sudden collapse. This was a phenomenon characterized by strength, beneficence and endurance. It fulfilled to a pre-eminent degree the needs and yearnings of the human body, intellect and soul. It changed the course of human history. It flung wide open the gates of progress in all directions. Its impact continues to be felt today, perhaps more widely and strongly than at any time since the first three or four centuries of the Muslim era.

What is the secret of this strength and endurance? This is the question to which Dr. Vaglieri supplies an answer in her very valuable book. She brings to her task wide scholarship and deep sincerity, sympathy and understanding. These qualities have led her unerringly to the true answer and she has not hesitated to state it in clear terms. Her book is concise but covers a wide field. Within a brief compass, Professor Vaglieri has succeeded in compressing a penetrating survey of the principal aspects of Islam. Through the

10

presentation of Islam with such understanding Professor Vaglieri has not only laid the West under a heavy debt of gratitude, she has also won the affectionate admiration of the Muslim world.

This does not mean that on points of detail the author's thesis will find unanimous support among all sections of Muslims. Such differences of approach and appraisal, however, do not detract from the value of her great contribution.

While presenting her appreciation of the teachings of Islam and the life and character of the Prophet of Islam, Dr. Vaglieri has not failed to lay her finger boldly upon one of the principal causes of the decline of the Muslims and the disintegration of Muslim society in modern times. She has also indicated the remedy:

> It is to the Holy Book which has never been altered at the hands either of its friends or its enemies, by either the learned or the unlettered, the book that time does not wear out but which remains just as it was revealed by God to the rough and simple Apostle, the last of all law-bearing Prophets—it is to this pure source that the Muslims will return. As they drink directly from this Holy Book, they will not fail to be re-invigorated.

How could it be otherwise? The Quran is the direct verbal revelation vouchsafed by God to Muhammad. It is literally the Word of God. Like the universe, also the creation of God, it possesses the quality of continuous life. It yields healthy and life-sustaining fruit in all ages.

Professor Vaglieri has the distinction of being alone among Western scholars in prescribing this remedy for the manifold ills that have befallen the Muslims in recent times. She is logically and inevitably led to this conclusion by her main thesis. Nonetheless it is a further proof of her profound insight into the life-giving qualities of the ever-fresh spring of all-embracing guidance which is the Quran. The Quran itself offers the same diagnosis and prescribes the same remedy. For instance, it says: (On that day) the Messenger will say, 'My Lord, my people indeed treated this Quran as a thing discarded'. [1]

The neglect of the guidance contained in the Quran is the cause: recourse to that guidance is the remedy.

The credit for making this most valuable little work available in English belongs to Dr. Aldo Caselli. Translation is never an easy task. When the sources of the subject matter are contained in an unfamiliar language and a work based on these sources has to be translated into a third language, the difficulties of translation are multiplied manifold. The transition from idiom to idiom alone presents a formidable problem. In the present case the original work, dealing as it does in compressed form with the gravest and most delicate topics, demands in the translation a certain amount of explanatory expansion while retaining strict fidelity to the text. Dr. Caselli has achieved this combination with excellent effect.

Responsible statesmen all over the world are diligently exploring means of promoting international understanding and good will. The most important problem they are confronted with is the so-called ideological conflict. For approximately four hundred million people, spread from Morocco to China and the Philippines, Islamic values form the basis of an ideology which they are anxious

---

[1] The Holy Quran, *Surah* 25, Verse 31.

All references of the Holy Quran, heretofore, have been given only by the number of the *Surah* (chapter) and the verses. The text of the English translation used throughout this book is the one published under the title, *The Holy Quran: Arabic Text and English Translation*, (Washington D. C., The American Fazl Mosque, 1955).

to promote and foster. They are convinced that these values furnish the most beneficent standards for healthy, prosperous and progressive life in all spheres.

Large sections of these people have just emerged or are in the process of emerging from a state of political dependence in which they have been subject to the control and domination of one or other of the European Colonial Powers. They are now in a position to review the situation, domestic and international, in which they find themselves and to carry out the needed adjustments. With international peace so precariously balanced between the Great Powers, the contribution which the Muslim peoples may be in a position to make towards maintaining and strengthening it, may prove to be decisive. Each day that passes emphasizes the increasing importance of this contribution and consequently the vital need of sympathetic understanding and appreciation of the source which, in the last resort, will mould their thinking, their policies and their actions.

Western scholars and writers have in recent years shown an increasing awareness of the need of sympathy, understanding and appreciation in their approach towards Islam. But prejudices which have been fostered during long centuries will take time to be overcome. Sustained and strenuous effort is needed to substitute in their place an attitude of objective appreciation.

Another difficulty is that the West bas been only too prone to attribute the faults and weaknesses of the Muslims of today to the teachings and influence of Islam, rather than to the ignorance of the mass of the Muslims of the true Islamic values and their neglect of them.

In all these respects, Professor Vaglieri's admirable little volume fills an urgent need. Muslims and non-Muslims alike can derive great benefit from its perusal. Readers of English will also appreciate Dr. Caselli's labour of love in making the text available in English.

An Interpretation of Islam should be widely read. It will prove of the utmost value in promoting friendly understanding between the Muslims and the West, and thus strengthening international peace.

Islam is universal in its appeal. The values taught by Islam will be joyfully acclaimed in the West, once they are properly understood. Professor Vaglieri's work will be welcomed as one of the great pioneers in opening the way towards that consummation.

ZAFRULLA KHAN

The Hague:

February 25, 1957

CHAPTER 1

The Rapid Spread of Islam

Islam, like a spring of pure and refined water, developed among barbarian people in a desolate and arid land far from the crossroads of civilization and human thought. So abundant was its volume that the spring fast became a creek, then a river, and finally overflowed and broke into thousands of channels, spilling out over the country. In those places where the miraculous water was sampled, people who had become divided were brought together again and disagreements were settled; and in place of the blood feud which was the supreme law and which served to keep together tribes of the same origin, a new sentiment began to make itself felt: a sentiment of brotherhood among men bound together by common ideals of morality and religion. As soon as this spring became an irresistible river, its pure and vigorous stream encircled mighty kingdoms representing old civilizations, and, before their peoples could realize the true import of the event, it overtook them, levelling countries, demolishing barriers, waking slumbering minds with its noise and making a united community out of the widest variety of nations.

Such a phenomenon had never before been witnessed in history. It is difficult to appreciate the speed with which Islam accomplished its conquests and changed from the religion of a few enthusiasts to that of millions of men. It is still a puzzle to the human mind to discover what were the secret forces which enabled rough warriors to triumph over people so far their superiors in civilization, wealth, experience and ability to wage war. It is surprising how these people could occupy so much territory and then consolidate their conquests in such a way that even centuries of warfare did not succeed in dislodging them; how they could inspire the souls of their followers with so much zeal for their ideals, preserve a pulsating vitality unknown to other religions, even ten centuries after the death of Muhammad; and infuse into the minds of their followers, although of an age and culture quite different from that of the first Muslims, a burning faith capable of any sacrifice.

Islam, which during the Meccan period of Muhammad's ministry had been exclusively concerned with making an earnest appeal on behalf of monotheism, became, after the emigration of the Prophet and his followers to Medina, a powerful political force. Muhammad, the patient victim of the sarcasm and persecution of the Quraysh, having been invested by God with the mission of defending himself from his enemies, was compelled to take up the sword and was thenceforth granted no respite by his enemies which could permit him to put it down.

Not even two years had elapsed from that memorable day when God granted the sorely persecuted Muslims permission to oppose force by force, which marks the beginning of the ascendancy of Islam and of a real social and political revolution, when the followers of Muhammad won their first battle over the people of Mecca. From that day, except for a few, perhaps inevitable checks, Islam witnessed an unbroken series of encounters, battles and conquests in the religions as well as in the political fields. In the eighth year these culminated in an event of surpassing importance, namely, the conquest of Mecca itself. [1]

Arab warriors left their deserts and moved across the boundaries into Palestine and further North into Syria. A great expedition against Syria from where the next attack was apprehended, was about to be prepared when the voice of the Prophet, which had caused such intense excitement in so many human hearts, and which was soon to make such a strong appeal to more distant peoples, was stilled forever in death in the eleventh year of the Hegira.

Arabia was now unified. The disruptive activities of the Bedouins, who tried to revive the anarchy of the pre-Islamic period, did not achieve their objective, being defeated and overcome by the government at Medina. This may well be claimed the first miracle of the new religion: a country which for centuries had been the field of continuous and fratricidal battles, at last knew security and peace!

The passage in the Quran which refers to the universality of Islam as the religion sent by God to his Prophet as "a mercy for all peoples" [2] is a direct appeal to the worlds. [3] This is definite proof that the Prophet felt with an absolute certainty that his mission was to go beyond the limits of the Arab nation and that he was to convey the new Word to people of different races and languages. Evidence of the same consciousness is also found in the tradition

---

[1] The custom of making *razzias* has been considered a legitimate form of warfare in Arabia since the most remote times, and is not to be judged by concepts prevailing in modern European society.

[2] *Surah* 21, Verse 108.

[3] See *Surah* 12, Verse 105; *Surah* 38, Verse 88; *Surah* 68, Verse 53; *Surah* 81, Verse 28, where the word "worlds" is construed as meaning humanity in the larger sense.

which mentions that it was a custom of Muhammad's to address himself to "the red and to the black ones", or to employ other similar expressions. Further evidence is furnished by the mention of future conquests beyond the boundaries of Arabia, and finally in the contacts which Muhammad himself began to make with foreign countries.

The Caliphs who succeeded Muhammad as Heads of the Islamic State, being the faithful interpreters of his thinking, followed the road which he had opened, and carried the flag of Islam to the center of Asia on the East and to the Atlantic Ocean on the West.

Sixteen years had elapsed since the Hegira [4] when the Persian empire, which for centuries had fought against the Byzantine Empire without either one destroying the other, broke up beyond recovery at the Battle of Quadisiyya. The fleeing king went from province to province, up to the extreme boundaries of the empire, and died in the thirty-first year of the Hegira. The Persian empire became Arab territory.

In the meantime, the occupation of Palestine and Syria was completed. These countries could be considered definitely in Arab hands by the Islamic year 19. In the year 21, the victorious army pushed itself up to Mosul, in the center of Armenia. A fleet was built and an annual expedition set sail from the harbour of Syria in Asia-Minor to carry the war to the very Capital of the Byzantine Empire. In the year 18, the first Arab army appeared in Egypt, and in the year 21 Alexandria capitulated: in the year 23, Tripoli was conquered, and in 27 the first important expedition was undertaken against South Tunisia. But why go on listing these dates? The army

---

[4] Literally: "migration". It indicates the departure on June 20, 622, of Muhammad from Mecca. The Muslim era starts with that event.

moved fast, battles followed each other, success seemed to give wings to the feet of the conquerors: the Caliphates of Abu Bakr (13 a.h.), of Omar (23 a.h.), of Othman (35 a.h.) resounded with the joyful news of wonderful victories. These were followed by the organization and consolidation of the conquered territories, which was an achievement not less marvellous than the conquests themselves.

Two civilizations and two religions having been demolished, a new stream of intense life began to flow in the veins of these exhausted peoples. There unfolded before the eyes of an astonished world a new religion, a simple, easy, one which speaks to the heart and to the brain; a new form of government, far superior in its moral principles and qualities to those existing at that time, was established; gold that had been hidden in the safes of plutocrats began changing bands and going to the poor, starting a system of healthy circulation once again; educated, capable, intelligent men under the guidance of a government ruled by honest, democratic ideals found encouragement in the new order and were able to rise to the highest public offices. It is safe to say that after a few inevitable excesses by soldiers during the invasions, a new era of prosperity and wealth was ushered in, a richness which Asia had not witnessed for centuries. The life of the conquered peoples, their civil rights and wealth received a degree of protection approximating to that enjoyed by the Muslims themselves.

Disturbed by such a profound political and religious trans-formation, men asked themselves what had brought it about? But many of them were blind or purposely closed their eyes, wandering long and hopelessly in a labyrinth of wrong conjectures. They could not realize that only a holy force could have supplied the first impulse for such a vast movement. They did not want to believe that the wisdom of God alone was responsible for the mission of Muhammad, the last of the great law-bearing Prophets, the one who forever concluded their series. Such a mission had to be a universal mission for all mankind without distinction of nationality, country or race. They were either blind or did not want to see. These people went on spreading the word that the essence of Islam was violent aggression. They claimed it was a religion imposed by the sword; they charged it with intolerance. They accused Muhammad himself of lying, of cruelty and of lust. They tried to demolish his admirable work of social and religious reform. They tried to make the devotion of his companions and followers appear as selfish interest, and represented them as people animated only by a desire for wealth and worldly prosperity.

We must first of all consider this charge of the "aggressive spirit of Islam". If by it is meant that Muhammad, as distinct from the founders of other religions, used his sword and organized military expeditions, looking to further distant successes and conquests, and that his example was imitated by his followers, then we must say that this is true; but we must also search with an equally open mind why this had to be. If the charge is that a destructive war was the necessary way to impose the faith, and that the need of conquests was an essential part of the very nature of the Islamic religion, then we must reject the accusation, for we can prove, using as evidence the Quran and the actions of Muhammad himself, that this is entirely false.

The Prophet, as one inspired, used to speak to the people of Mecca and tell them of his celestial visions, which demanded of him the patient bearing of injuries and aroused the distrust of the Quraysh. When he made the difficult decision to migrate to Medina and thus became the center of a political struggle, he had to choose between dying ignominiously, which would have been against the wishes of God, and fighting to save himself and his small community from ruin. The struggle was between anarchy, the materialism of barbarian pagans, and the disagreements and falsehoods of the highly civilized but intolerant Jews on the one hand, and a high ideal of religious and social regeneration on the other.

This was the ideal which Muhammad desired at any cost to achieve and he fought as only a meek one could fight against arrogance, as one who has little will to fight is compelled to fight against those who are bent upon his destruction by force. This he did with very little help, but with the certainty that he was opening the way for carrying the truth to many lives, and that he was charged to indicate the right road in the midst of darkness. Arriving in Medina, he had first of all lent his friendly hand to the Jews, who in this city represented a rich and flourishing group. He invited them to loyal cooperation in political and social unity. But when he realized that they were utterly hostile to him and that they were bent upon the pursuit of a false and traitorous course, he had to fight and punish them. War against external enemies was a necessity of the times; no Arab of the desert could adapt himself to a condition of permanent peace, having been accustomed for centuries to wage war as a normal pursuit. Consequently, once Muhammad had settled internal conflicts, he had to face the hostility of the Quraysh and of those tribes which were not yet in treaty relations with him. But war with its risks and military triumphs helped to cement the new community. It furnished the necessary means of survival for the companions who had migrated with the Prophet from Mecca to Medina. It satisfied the natural propensities of the Bedouins; and in a barbarian milieu which was rendered attractive by dangers, boldness and adventures, it represented a means of safeguarding life and of facilitating the fulfilment of the Prophet's mission. War was always a means of safeguarding and exalting the true faith and not an end in itself; it was a necessary defence, not an unjust offence.

The Quran clearly expressed this idea:

And fight in the cause of Allah against those who fight against you, but do not transgress. Surely, Allah loves not the transgressors. [5]

And fight them until there is no persecution, and religion is *freely professed* for Allah. But if they desist, then *remember* that no hostility is allowed except against the aggressors. [6]

To deny that the Muslims pushed their conquests by a certain spirit of aggression, would certainly be to exhibit an extreme ignorance of human nature. But is it really right to blame this on their religion? Once they had discovered their strength and the weakness of their opponents, what power on earth could have stopped their impetuosity and kept them within the limits of the law? Nevertheless even at the peak of their power and triumph, the victorious Arabs were always ready to tell their enemies: "Give up the fighting, pay a modest tax, and we will grant you full protection; or accept Islam, become a member of our community, and you will have the same rights as we have ourselves".

If we look into the prophecies of Muhammad or at the first Muslim conquests, it is easy to see how false was the accusation that Islam was imposed by the sword and that only by such means could its rapid and wide diffusion be accounted for. The Quran says:

There should be no compulsion in Religion. Surely, right has become distinct from wrong; so whosoever refuses to be led by those who transgress, and believes in Allah, has surely grasped a strong handle which knows no breaking. And Allah is All-Hearing, All-Knowing. [7]

---

[5] *Surah* 2, Verse 191.
[6] *Surah* 2, Verse 194.
[7] **Surah** 2, Verse 257.

> And say, '*It is* the truth from your Lord;
> wherefore let him who will, believe, and let him
> who will, disbelieve.' [8]

Muhammad, always following these divine principles, was very tolerant, particularly towards the followers of monotheistic religions. He knew how to show patience with the pagans, always waiting in the belief that time would complete his work of conversion. He was satisfied with what we would call a purely formal conversion of the Bedouins, because he knew that these sons of the desert were impatient by nature of checks of any kind. He well knew that God would finally enter into the human heart.

"Why do you want to push men to believe when faith can only come from God?" he said one day to one of his followers. At the time when the verses which deal with tolerance were revealed, he was not a dreamer followed by a small group of dreamers like him, nor a philosopher paralyzed by his awareness of a diversity of forces, but rather a man in the fullness of his strength at the head of a highly organized state, commanding goad, obedient soldiers whom he could always have used against anyone.

The history of the first decades of Islam provides us with several examples of the religious tolerance shown by the first Caliphs towards followers of monotheistic religions. Just as the Prophet himself gave guarantees to the Christians of Nejran that their Christian institutions would be preserved and gave orders to the head of an expedition to Yemen that no Jews be molested in his Judaism, so the Caliphs gave similar instructions to their generals on the conduct of their armies in war. These triumphant generals followed Muhammad's example in making agreements with the conquered peoples. By virtue of these agreements, the conquered were granted the freedom of following the old religion and

---

[8] *Surah* 18, Verse 30.

traditions, provided that those who did not accept Islam would pay the government a fair tax, *jizya*. This tax was lighter than the taxes which the Muslims were liable to pay to their own government. In return these subjects (called *Dhimmi)* were granted protection not different from that enjoyed by the Muslim community itself. Consequently, as the practices followed by the Prophet and by the first orthodox Caliphs became law itself for later Muslims, it is no exaggeration to insist that Islam was not satisfied with preaching religious tolerance, but that it made tolerance a part of its religious law.

Once agreements with the defeated peoples were made, the Muslims left them freedom of religion and did not use violence to compel conversions. The Muslim armies were not followed by a troop of insistent and unwanted preachers, nor did they place preachers in specially favoured positions to expound or defend their creed. On the contrary, at one period they imposed a practice on the Muslim neophytes which certainly did not help to facilitate the spread of Islam, namely, the requirement to present themselves before the quadi and to declare that their conversion was not the result of any pressure and that it had no wordly gain as its object. During the time of the Omayyad Caliphs, there was even an attempt to stop the stream of conversions, which was somewhat embarrassing from the economic point of view since the loss of the *jizya* was causing a diminution in revenue from taxes. Not only were Jews and Christians left to live in peace without any questioning of their religious beliefs, but they were named to offices in the government when their personal qualifications were of such a nature as to attract the notice of the rulers. Certain restrictions imposed on Christians and Jews in the matter of freedom of religion, certain rules requiring the carrying of visible signs designed to mark them out as Jews or Christians, prohibitions against the building of new churches or the repairing of old ones— these are incidents of later periods which were more marked by fanaticism, when nations other than the Arabs imported a certain tendency towards bigotry into Islam.

Of course, it cannot be denied that even Muslims, like the followers of all other religions, exhibited some of those flames of passion which kindle hate and spread blood. But we must realize that these had their first cause in facts external to the religion of Islam itself and that Islam had the effect of quieting them down in order to make room for mildness and benevolence. It must also be admitted that Islam was not spared its share of conflict among the various Islamic sects, a conflict which carried in its wake inevitable persecutions; but for this as well, the main explanation is to be found in political or dynastic rivalries. Islam itself furnishes no justification or warrant for them.

Blinded by hate, the most powerful enemies of Islam have sought to smear the Prophet of God with calumnious charges. They forget that Muhammad before he began his mission was highly esteemed by his own countrymen for integrity of conscience and purity of life. Nor do these people stop to ask themselves how could it be that Muhammad could have threatened liars and hypocrites with the eternal fire in the burning words of the Quran if he himself had been a liar. How could he have dared to preach, in spite of the insults of his countrymen, if he, a man of simple nature, had not been continuously urged on by inner forces? How could he have started a struggle which looked hopeless? How could he have carried it on for over ten years at Mecca with very little success and countless sorrows, if he had not the very deep conviction of the truth of his mission? How could so many noble and intelligent Muslims have believed in him and thrown in their lot with him, joined the new faith and consequently associated themselves with a society made up for the most part of slaves, freedmen and indigent people if they had not felt in his word the sincerity of the Truth? We do not need to say more, for even among Occidentals the truth is well accepted that the sincerity of Muhammad was deep and true.

Against the accusation of cruelty the answer is easy. Muhammad, Head of a State, defender of the life and freedom of his people, in the exercise of justice punished severely individuals guilty of crimes, and this attitude of his has to be considered in the light of his times and also in the light of the wild and barbarian society in which he lived. Muhammad, as a preacher of the religion of God, was gentle and merciful even towards his personal enemies. In him were blended justice and mercy, two of the noblest qualities which the human mind can conceive. It is not difficult to support this with many examples that are to be found in his biographies. One of his biographers says, "War, this horrible necessity of human life, was in practice made less cruel by him." Another reports that he was accustomed to giving this order to his soldiers: "Spare the aged, the women, and the children; refrain from demolishing the homes of those who do not resist you; do not destroy their means of subsistence; do not destroy fruit-bearing trees; do not touch palm trees."

In another chapter we shall deal with the accusation of licentiousness, as well as show how noble and sublime the work of this reformer really was, this reformer who, within the span of a few years, transformed a welter of idolatrous and barbarous people into a united monotheistic community, which was animated by the highest moral sentiments. The facts will also refute the point of view of those who see in the greater number of Muhammad's followers only egotistical speculators and greedy robbers, pushed towards his party by a desire for spoils and conquest. It would occupy us far too long to cite instances which testify to the brilliant ardour, the unbounded pity, the devoted zeal of the majority of his followers. Suffice it to say that there are certain kinds of conflicts which cannot be won unless there is present a very powerful moral factor, an abiding faith in the justice of the cause—and this factor Islam possessed.

Having dealt briefly with the accusations which are most commonly advanced against Islam, let us face the question: How can it be explained that in spite of the great freedom of religion granted in the Islamic nations to non-Muslim citizens, and in the absence of any real missionary organization, Islam continues to make progress in Asia and Africa in the face of the widespread decline of religion in recent years? Today, it cannot be said that the sword of the conqueror paves the way—on the contrary, in regions which once were Muslim states, new governments of other religions are in power and strong missionary organizations have been working among the Muslims over long periods—and yet they have not succeeded in removing Islam from the life of the Muslim peoples.

What miraculous strength is hidden in this religion? What inner power of persuasion is blended in it? From what depths of the human soul does its appeal evoke a stirring response?

CHAPTER II

The Simplicity of Islamic Dogma

Islam approaches the individual with a two-fold invitation; to believe that there is only one God and that Muhammad is sent by God.

The Arabic prophet, with a voice which was inspired by a deep communion with his Master, preached the purest monotheism to the worshippers of fetish and the followers of a corrupt Christianity and Judaism. He put himself in open conflict with those regressive tendencies of mankind which lead to the association of other beings with the Creator.

> Say, 'He is Allah, the One;
> 'Allah, the Independent and Besought of all.
> 'He begets not, nor is He begotten;
> 'And there is none like unto Him.' [1]

---

[1] *Surah* 112, Verses 2-5.

In order to lead men to a belief in one God, he did not delude them with tales of happenings which deviate from the normal course of nature—the so-called miracles; nor did he compel them to keep quiet by using celestial threats which only undermine man's ability to think. Rather, he simply invited them, without asking them to leave the realm of reality, to consider the universe and its laws. Being confident of the resultant belief in the one and indispensable God, he simply let men read in the book of life. Muhammad Abduh and Ameer Ali both state that Muhammad was content to appeal to the intimate conscience of the individual and to the intuitive judgment of man.

> And your God is One God; there is no God but He, the Gracious, the Merciful.

> Verily, in the creation of the heavens and the earth and in the alternation of night and day, and in the ships which sail in the sea with that which profits men, and in the water which Allah sends down from the sky and quickens therewith the earth after its death and scatters therein all kinds of beasts, and in the change of the winds, and the clouds pressed into service between the heaven and the earth—are indeed Signs for the people who understand.

> And there are some among men who take for themselves objects of worship other than Allah, loving them as they should love Allah. [2]

There is more than one passage in the Quran which invites the reader to take into consideration the testimony offered by nature.

---

[2] *Surah 2, Verses 164-166.*

I shall quote only some verses from the chapter known as "The Merciful".

> And He has set the earth for *His* creatures;
> Therein are *all kinds of* fruit and palm-trees with sheaths,
> And grain with *its* husk and fragrant plants.
> Which, then, of the favours of your Lord will you twain deny, O *men and Jinn?*
> He created man from dry ringing clay *which is* like baked pottery.
> And the Jinn He created from the flame of fire.
> Which, then, of the favours of your Lord will you twain deny?
> The Lord of the two Easts and the Lord of the two Wests!
> Which, then, of the favours of your Lord will you twain deny?
> He has made the two bodies of water flow. They will *one day* meet.
> Between them is *now a* barrier; they encroach not *one upon the other.*
> Which, then, of the favours of your Lord will you twain deny?
> There come out from them pearls and coral.
> Which, then, of the favours of your Lord will you twain deny?
> And His are the lofty ships reared aloft on the sea like mountains.
> Which, then, of the favours of your Lord will you twain deny? [3]

---

[3] *Surah* 55, Verses 11-26.

Thanks to Islam, paganism in its various forms was defeated. The concept of the universe, the practices of religion, and the customs of social life were each liberated from all the monstrosities which had degraded them, and human minds were made free of prejudice. Man finally realized his dignity. He humbled himself before the Creator, the Master of all mankind; he not only could say, but as a matter of fact had to say, with Abraham:

> I have turned my face toward Him who created the Heavens and the Earth, being ever inclined to God, and I am not one of those who associate gods with God. [4]

And with Muhammad:

> My prayers and my sacrifice and my life and my death are *all* for Allah, the Lord of the Worlds.
> He has no partner. And so am I commanded, and I am the first of those who submit. [5]

The spirit was liberated from prejudice, man's will was set free from the ties which had kept it bound to the will of other men, or other so-called hidden powers. Priests, false guardians of mysteries, brokers of salvation, all those who pretended to be mediators between God and man and consequently believed they had authority over other people's wills, fell from their pedestals. Man became the servant of God alone and towards other men he had only the obligations of one free man towards other free men. While previously men had suffered from the injustices of social differences, Islam proclaimed equality among human beings. Each Muslim was distinguished from other Muslims not by reason of birth or any other factor not connected with his personality, but

---

[4] *Surah* 6, Verse 80.
[5] *Surah* 6, Verses 163-164.

only by his fear of God, his good deeds, his moral and intellectual qualities.

The Quran states:

> O mankind, We have created you from a male and a female; and We have divided you into tribes and sub-tribes that you may recognize one of another. Verily, the most honourable among you, in the sight of Allah, is he who is the most righteous among you. [6]

A tradition says:

> With Islam, God has caused the disappearance of pride, which was a characteristic of pagans, and of their habit of talking about their fathers: because man was born of Adam, and Adam of dust. According to God, the noblest of men is the one who is most fearful of Him.

Islam swept away the secrecy with which others had shrouded the study of sacred scriptures, reproaching those who were only able to recite the words and comparing those who claimed to be the repositories of the Pentateuch to a donkey loaded with books. It invited any man of religious sentiments to acquire the knowledge that was necessary for understanding God's word. Among the Muslims, there was no duly authorized exegesis of the holy book on which they were required to base their beliefs. Nor were there councils or synods which, after discussion, presumed to lay down the precise formula which was to be considered as the living symbol of orthodoxy. Islam did not grant to any one of its followers the right to pass judgment on the faith of another brother.

---

[6] *Surah* 49, Verse 14.

The Quran had said:

> O ye who believe! let not one people deride
> *another* people, who may be better than they. [7]

And tradition has fully established the idea that the acceptance of a believer's faith and deeds is God's privilege denying to any servant of God the right to pass judgment on another servant's piety by his approval or disapproval. Later on, when theological studies degenerated into subtle scholarly discussions, followers of different schools accused each other of misbelief and attempted to persuade the civil government to determine the penalties to be imposed on heterodoxy. In the fifth century of the Islamic era, thanks to a great thinker of Islam, Al-Ghazali, a doctrine was proclaimed that agreement on the principal dogmas of faith was the only basis for recognizing men as believers, and that differences in respect of dogmatic or ritual details could not provide any basis for exclusion. "You must stop condemning those people who, in their prayers, face towards Mecca." This was the rule laid down by the philosopher. It at once rendered valueless any dogmatic speciousness, any formulae which pretended to be the only ones through which salvation could be achieved; and Islamic society was restored to that open minded spirit of tolerance which had been an essential characteristic of the early Muslims and which, because of a false interpretation of the spirit of religion, was in danger of disappearing.

The God of Islam, One in His essence, in His attributes, and in His acts, is an all-mighty God, Judge of the Universe and Master of the day of judgment. He will call to Him all those who have not treated His call with sarcasm or contempt, and who were able to rise from the materiality of their personalities and their earthly belongings, to the sentiment of utter dependence upon the Creator.

---

[7] *Surah* 49, Verse 12.

In the earliest *Surahs* of the Quran, God's inspiration is expressed in eschatological representations. Woe to those who do not repent and do not submit themselves to God. Terrible punishments, very painful indeed, await them. Woe to those who dare to resist or despise the guidance of Prophets sent to them. God will exterminate them. He is the one who knows everything, sees everything, hears everything. He is the Creator of Heaven and earth, of life and death. He is the Master of the Throne. His knowledge is perfect. His will is absolute; His power irresistible. All these qualities are revealed by His own works. While everything needs Him, He depends only upon things originated by Him. He does not resemble any one of His creatures; His only connection with them is that He created them; they belong to Him and they will come back to Him. But this very powerful God is also a just God. An unjust God cannot be conceived. He knows about the most insignificant good deed done by any one of His creatures and He will not allow it to be lost; He will not do the smallest injustice to anyone, not even as small as the fibre which goes to make up the stone of the date. [8]

Muslim and Christian theologians have often asked themselves how to answer the problem of man's free will. Different solutions have been offered, according to the sect to which the theologian belonged, but all answers hinge on the preceding axiom of divine justice and on other statements found in the Quran, to the effect that man's actions, whether good or bad, are the result of his complete freedom. Muhammad Abduh states that fairly early in Islam such a feeling of dependence in all fields of human consciousness began to develop that a favourable climate was created for the triumph of the negation of the free will; virtues and vices, crimes and punishments were all regarded as due solely to God's will, man's will had dropped out of consideration. Today, on the contrary, the majority of Muslims, apart from a few relatively unimportant groups, have

---

[8] See *Surah* 4, Verse 50.

reverted to the idea of laying responsibility for action back on a man's own conscience.

God does not bar His road to anyone, not even to the wrong-doers; He bestows upon all the power and the capacity to perform good deeds. Those expressions in the Quran which could be construed as contradicting this idea, can be explained when we fully understand their true import. Man in his relation to God can be compared to the traveller who makes a mistake in the desert while searching for the correct road to take him to his final destination. The one who, thanks to his faith and good deeds, is deserving of God's mercy and benevolence will be rewarded by God with guidance while God will leave alone the one who does not occupy himself with good deeds; God will not stretch His arm towards him, but at the same time He will not be the one who puts him on the evil road.

This omnipotent God, ready to punish, is also the Merciful, the Guardian of His servants, the Defender of the orphan, the Guide of the sinner, the Liberator from pain, the Friend of the poor, the generous and ready-to-forgive Master. He listens; He grants favours because well-being is in His hands.

God's mercy is one of the most frequent themes of the Quran; the attributes, *Ar-Rahman, Ar-Rahim*— "the Merciful", "the Clement" with which each chapter begins virtually represent the basic themes of the entire text.

God's blessing is assured to the sinner who repents; even the wrongdoer may hope for it, for, although God can overtake with His punishment anyone He wishes, His mercy "encompasses everything", and because He himself has commanded that mercy shall be an unbreakable law. [9]

---

[9] *Surah* 7, Verse 157.

This accords perfectly with what tradition brings to us:

> When God had perfected the creation, He wrote in the book which He kept near Him: 'My mercy triumphs over my anger'.

> God divided mercy into one hundred parts; He kept ninety-nine of them for Himself and released one for the world; from that alone comes all the grace which mankind enjoys.

Among the divine attributes we find that of love. The Quran says:

> If ye love Allah, follow me: *then* will Allah love you and forgive you your faults. And Allah is Most Forgiving, Merciful. [10]

But this is not enough. In a collection of the forty most important traditional sayings, we find this revelation of God to Muhammad: "By means of freely supporting charitable institutions, My servant will more and more approach Me so that I will love him, and when I love him, I am his eye, his ear, his tongue, his hand; thanks to Me he will see, hear, speak, walk."

We doubt if this concept of God, composed of all the most perfect qualities, and purified from all the imperfect ones, would appear as noble and elevated to everyone. Certainly it would be said that it is not original, that it is too much like the Jewish and the Christian concepts, and that no new element has been introduced by Islam to illustrate the relationship between man and God. But what value would such criticism have if we realize that Muhammad himself did not claim to bring new ideas but explicitly declared that

---

[10] *Surah* 3, Verse 32.

he had been sent by God to restore the religion of Abraham, corrupted by those who came after, and to reconfirm what God had already revealed to preceding prophets like Moses, Isaiah, Jesus Christ? He was but the last of the lawbearing prophets.

Islam came at a time when people were divided into religious sects, when they were fighting and cursing each other, each sect believing itself to be the sole repository of the word of God—at a time when fighting and fanaticism were considered a necessary part of religious life. Islam came and proclaimed that religion had at all times, and by the mouths of all the prophets, been simply one—that in essence it had taught always the same things; to hold God alone in His sovereignty, to submit to His will, and to obey His commandments, practising good and keeping away from evil. Furthermore, Islam insisted that the variety of forms and rituals which different religions presented, proceeded from the mercy of God, Who gave to each people in each particular time a religion suited to its needs and susceptible of development along with the progress of the human mind; but it insisted that at last, when mankind had been prepared by events and had reached a state of maturity and was in a position to comprehend a divine Teaching, which appealed not only to the emotions but also to the intellect, Muhammad had appeared to reconcile all these teachings for the benefit of humanity, to settle the differences between the "people of the book", which means Christians and Jews, and to guide men towards the attainment of happiness both in this life and in the one beyond.

All Muslims agree that faith in God comes from faith in the Prophets. We could not have faith in the Prophets or in the words of a revealed book, if these had not been preceded by the certainty in the human soul of the existence of God and by the probability that He might send Prophets bearing His guidance. Consequently, the first duty of man is to consider the phenomena of nature and to meditate upon them in order to arrive at the certainty of the existence of God. Starting from this fundamental, there is then developed faith in the Prophets and in the revealed books. In its revealed book Islam has something of the miraculous.

The miracle of Islam *par excellence* is the Quran, through which a constant and unbroken tradition transmits to us news of an absolute certainty. This is a book which cannot be imitated. Each of its expressions is a comprehensive one, and yet it is of proper size, neither too long nor too short. Its style is original. There is no model for this style in Arab literature of the times preceding it. The effect which it produces on the human soul is obtained without any adventitious aid through its own inherent excellences. The verses are equally eloquent all through the text, even when they deal with topics, such as commandments and prohibitions, which must necessarily affect its tone. Stories of Prophets, descriptions of the beginning and the end of the world, enumerations and expositions of the divine attributes are repeated but repeated in a way which is so impressive that they do not weaken the effect. The text proceeds from one topic to another without losing its power. Depth and sweetness, qualities which generally do not go together, are found together here, where each rhetoric figure finds a perfect application. How could this marvellous book be the work of Muhammad, an illiterate Arab who in all his life composed only two or three verses, none of which reveals the least poetic quality, e.g. "I am the Prophet and do not lie. I am the son of Abd el-Muttalib."?

Although the opponents of Islam were invited by Muhammad to compose a book similar to his own, or, at least, a chapter ("And if you are in doubt as to what We have sent down to Our servant, then produce a chapter like it;"), [11] and although those who had the ability to express themselves with great eloquence were plentiful among the Arabs, yet nobody was able to produce anything which

---

[11] *Surah* 2, Verse 24.

could stand in comparison with the Quran; they 'fought the Prophet with arms but failed to match the excellence of the Quran'.

For the book, besides its perfection in form and method, proved itself beyond imitation even in its substance. In it, among other things, we read a forecast of future events, and a description of events which had taken place centuries before but were generally ignored. There are frequent references to the laws of nature, to various sciences, both religious and secular. We find there vast stores of knowledge which are beyond the capacity of the most intelligent of men, the greatest of philosophers and the ablest of politicians. For all these reasons the Quran could not be the work of an uneducated man, who had spent all his life in the midst of an unrefined society far away from men of learning and religion, a man who always insisted that he was but a man just like any other, and, as such, unable to perform miracles unless he had the help of Almighty God. The Quran could have its source only in Him Whose knowledge comprehends everything in heaven and earth.

We have still another proof of the divine origin of the Quran in the fact that its text has remained pure and unaltered through the centuries from the day of its delivery until today, and will remain so, God willing, as long as the universe continues to exist. Read over and over again all through the Muslim world, this work does not induce in the believer any sense of weariness. On the contrary, through repeated reading it endears itself more and more each day. It arouses a deep sense of reverence and awe in one who reads or hears it. It can be readily learned by heart, so that today, in spite of the low ebb of faith, thousands of people can repeat it by heart. In Egypt alone there are more *huffaz* [12] than there are people in all Europe who can recite the Gospels by heart.

It was not the use of force nor the efforts of insistent missionaries that brought about the rapid spread of Islam. Rather, it

---

[12] Plural *of Hafiz* (lit: Guardian) i.e. one who has learnt the Quran by heart.

was the fact that the Book which was presented by the Muslims to the conquered people, with freedom to accept or reject it, was the Book of God, the word of the Truth, the greatest miracle that Muhammad could have presented to the faltering ones on earth.

Apart from the two fundamental dogmas already mentioned, the unity of God and the mission of Muhammad, all other dogmas in which the Muslims believe and which are accepted by the Islamic community after centuries of study and debate, are not of such a nature as in any way to obstruct modern science or to raise opposition to philosophical truths. Concerning the Creation, the Quran, though it refers to the primordial state and to the origin of the world ("Do not the disbelievers see that the heavens and the earth were a closed-up *mass,* then we opened them out? And we made from water every living thing.") [13] does not put any limitation whatever upon the powers of the human mind, but leaves it free to go its own way. Concerning natural laws, it limits itself to stating that God has promulgated certain laws which rule the Creation and which do not change.

While all other religions prescribe for their followers a heavy load of doctrines which are hard both to carry and to understand, Islam is a religion of marvellous easiness and of crystal-clear simplicity. This was also another cause of its speedy diffusion at the time of the early conquests among people who had fallen into deep spiritual confusion on account of the uncertainty of some of their religious dogmas. It is also the cause of its continuous diffusion today among uncivilized peoples in Asia and Africa, for Islam can reach their souls without recourse to long explanations or involved sermons.

---

[13] *Surah* 21, Verse 31.

CHAPTER III

The Meaning of Islamic Rites

The foundations of Islam, apart from its testimony to the unity of God, are prayer, fasting, legal alms and the pilgrimage. All these rituals should be considered from more than the external point of view, for this would be as superficial as admiring shells without realizing that they are filled with precious pearls. Each of them has to be intimately examined in order to discover the secret which causes the spirit of the believer to be purified through them and gradually to lift itself towards God. Only then can we see that they have a double purpose—the exaltation of God by His servants, and the expression of their gratitude for the gifts bestowed by Him.

Called by the word of the Muezzin to fulfil their first religious duty, that of prayer, even those who are occupied with mundane affairs, are brought to a remembrance of their Creator. They begin the ritual by exalting God and they conclude it by offering Him their greetings. They always feel at ease in His presence. Humbling themselves with their foreheads to the ground, they express their absolute submission to the Divine Power. Words and acts in the

Islamic prayer each have a particular meaning, which is not so deep that it cannot be grasped by the average human mind.

This is not the place to enter into an exposition of them; we shall only say here that the disciplinary character of the various movements which accompany the words helps to keep the thoughts of the worshipper concentrated beyond the realm of the body, and enables him to express his devotion and to render thanks for Divine bounties in the most profound manner. The practice of facing in the direction of Mecca keeps alive in the Muslim world the memory of the glorious place which witnessed the birth of this regenerative faith, a holy centre around which at all times rotate the religious sentiments of the believers, all united in adoration of the same God.

The very high value of prayer as a means of moral elevation and purification of the heart is indicated by the Quran:

> Recite that which has been revealed to thee of the Book, and observe prayer. Surely, prayer restrains *one* from indecency and manifest evil, and remembrance of Allah indeed is the greatest *virtue*. And Allah knows what you do. [1]

God does not care for the formal observances of a form of cult, but He does demand the sincere devotion of the heart. This concept is clearly expressed in the Quran:

> Their flesh (i.e. of the animals slaughtered as sacrifice) reaches not Allah, nor does their blood, but it is your righteousness that reaches Him. [2]

---

[1] *Surah* 29, Verse 46.
[2] *Surah* 22, Verse 38.

Many are the traditions which confirm God's wishes in this matter: "A prayer in this Mosque of Medina," one of them says, "is worth a thousand prayers in any other mosque, with the exception of the sanctuary of Mecca; a prayer said there is worth one hundred thousand prayers recited in other mosques. But above all stands the value of the prayer which one pronounces in his own house where no one but God sees him and which has no other purpose than that of approaching God."

The prayer of the Muslim has not necessarily to be offered in a temple, for any place on earth, provided it is clean, is near to God and consequently fit for prayer, neither priests nor sacrifices nor ceremonies are needed to lift the heart of man towards his Creator.

For the prayer to be valid, only one condition is necessary— purity of the body, which also means purity of the soul, and that of the dress and the place. Islam reconsecrated the old habit of ablutions, using Muhammad's example for fixing the details of them and of the prayer. The Quran does not couple these practices of cult with any special prescription, so that an eminent modern writer, Ameer Ali, insists upon the marvellous simplicity and sobriety of the Quranic ritual which leaves the maximum of freedom in respect of the most elevated of spiritual functions.

The Friday service, which consists of a sermon and of prayers recited in common, also has its special advantages and significance. By bringing all Muslims together in the same ritual of humility and submission to the Lord, it makes them feel that they are all His creatures and thus brothers. The requirement that worshippers should follow the Imam, that is, the leader, in the act of the prayer, subjects them to a certain experience of discipline and obedience. Last of all, through the sermon, the Imam opens their hearts and lifts them to God.

The second "Pillar" of Islam is the institution of fasting, which, as is known, consists of abstention from eating, drinking and smoking and from marital intercourse during the hours of day-light all through the month of Ramadan. It is a practice of discipline, of mercy and of pity. It requires the believer to abstain from all the pleasures of the body during a certain period. It teaches him to curb his passions. By making him go hungry and to understand how painful this can be, it makes him have pity for the poor and the indigent. By making him appreciate what he has, it deepens his gratitude towards God. This compulsory fasting is prescribed for healthy and strong persons, is not asked of the weak, the sick, the traveller, the fighter for the cause of God, or the woman during her period, during child-bearing and while breast feeding a child. For God is not harsh towards His creatures and does not require acts of devotion which are beyond their strength.

All religions have recognized in some measure the great moral and social importance of giving alms and have recommended it as a tangible expression of charity, and as a suitable way to seek the benevolence of God. Only Islam, however, has the glory of having made it compulsory, translating into prescription and thus into reality, the teaching of Christ. Each Muslim is by law compelled to contribute a portion of his wealth for the benefit of the poor, those in need, the travellers, the strangers, etc. By fulfilling this religious duty, he experiences a deeper sense of humanity, purifies his soul of avarice, and begins to cherish hope of divine reward.

Each Muslim, if certain conditions are fulfilled, has the obligation to make a pilgrimage to Mecca at least once in his lifetime. The profound forces which are hidden in this prescription are of such a nature that the human mind can scarcely embrace them, yet those which are easily intelligible reveal perfect wisdom. No one can deny the advantage which comes to Islam through the annual reunion in one place of Muslims coming from all parts of the world: Arabs, Persians, Afghans, Indians, people from the Malay Peninsula, people from Maghrib and Sudan, and others all converge upon the sacred temple for the sole purpose of asking forgiveness from their merciful God. Meeting each other in such a place for such a purpose they forge new ties of love and brotherhood.

At least once in the life of a Muslim all differences between rich and poor, between beggar and Emir, are completely obliterated. For, during the period of the holy ceremonies, everyone wears the same very simple clothes, everyone leaves his own personal ornaments behind, and everyone has only one watchword, "*Allah-o-Akbar*" (God is great). The rituals which the pilgrims have to fulfill, such as going around the house of God *(Ka'ba),* the reunion near mount Arafat, and the sacrifice at Mina, awaken in him the remembrance of the great prophets and patriarchs of the past who have been in the same places. They bring to life again the deeds of Abraham, the founder of the pure religion, and of his son Ishmael and his wife Hagar. They awaken in the pilgrim the desire of imitating them in their compassion and their submission to the will of God.

God's wisdom is also made manifest in what we might call the limiting aspects of the rules relating to the pilgrimage, namely those prescribing the conditions under which the pilgrimage becomes obligatory. Those conditions are complete freedom of the individual, ability to pay the expenses involved, including the cost of transportation, the ability to support his dependents while the pilgrim is fulfilling his religious duty, and the feasibility and practicability of the trip.

In other words, Gad has not imposed on man the observance of a code too heavy for his strength, nor has He, in any one of the rituals, imposed inflexible, hard rules. For:

> Allah desires *to give* you facility and He desires not hardship for you. [3]

---

[3] *Surah* 2, Verse 186.

Allah desires not that He should place you in a difficulty, but He desires to purify you and to complete His favour upon you, so that you may be grateful. [4]

Allah burdens not any soul beyond its capacity. [5]

Allah desires to lighten your burden, for man has been created weak. [6]

All these principles, find confirmation in the tradition which says, "This religion is not a demanding one."

---

[4] *Surah* 5, Verse 7.
[5] *Surah* 2, Verse 287.
[6] *Surah* 4, Verse 29.

CHAPTER IV

Islamic Morale

Some Western writers have charged that Islamic morale is dangerous to the individual because it is full of that spirit of obedience and passive submission to the Divine which is implied in the name of Islam itself. A man, it is argued, who in the face of the Almighty has such a sense of dependence upon Him and places himself so completely in His bands, renouncing his own free will to Him, cannot have the same urge to do good as one who feels that he stands before God as the absolute master of his own conscience.

Before we try to present the high ethical concepts which enlighten the souls of Muhammad's followers, we shall answer this accusation with the words of a European scholar, Goldziher: ". . . As if the consciousness, so strong in the Muslim, of being submitted to an inflexible, divine law, or his faith in the transcendence of God were obstacles which would inhibit his approaching God through faith, virtue, good deeds, and being received in His mercy! As if the philosophical schematism of religions could modify the qualities of inner devotion of one who completely worships and who, being aware of his weakness and his impulses, humbly raises his spirit toward the omnipotent source of any strength and perfection whatsoever!".

Islam was not only not an obstacle to moral perfection; since it possessed in itself an efficient strength directed towards good deeds, it succeeded, earlier than other religions, in educating and raising men towards God. Islam succeeded because it was not less concerned for the moral responsibility of its members than other monotheistic religions whose prophets Muhammad recognized as his teachers, but in certain respects it was even more concerned than they, because it counted on human weakness and exhorted its believers towards ideals within their reach. The same virtues which Judaism and Christianity present as the supreme end of the moral life of man, are not only set forth but are even prescribed as ideals in Islam. This is true of the ideals of mercy towards all creatures, understanding, forgiveness, simplicity, fitness in social contacts, acceptance of misfortunes, and so on. Quranic statements stressing good deeds can be found by the thousand, but since we cannot spend too much time on this chapter, we shall present some of them selected at random:

> And what should make thee know what the ascent is?

> *It is* the freeing of a slave.
> Or feeding in a day of hunger.
> An orphan near of kin,
> Or a poor man *lying* in the dust. [1]

> So I warn you of a flaming Fire
> None shall enter it but the most wicked one,
> Who rejects *the truth* and turns *his* back.
> But the righteous *one* shall be kept away from it,

> Who gives his wealth to become purified.

---

[1] *Surah* 90, Verses 14-17.

And he owes no favour to anyone, which is to be repaid,

Except *that he gives his wealth* to seek the pleasure of his Lord, the Most High.
And soon will He be well pleased wi*th him* [2]

And they feed, for love of Him, the poor, the orphan, and the prisoner,

Saying, 'We feed you for Allah's pleasure *only.* We desire no reward nor thanks from you.[3]

And vie with one another in asking for forgiveness from your Lord, and for a Paradise whose price is the heavens and the earth, prepared for the God-fearing—

Those who spend in prosperity and adversity, and those who suppress anger and pardon men, and Allah loves those who do good; [4]

It is not righteousness that you turn your faces to the East or the West, but *truly* righteous is he who believes in Allah and the Last Day and the angels and the Book and the Prophets, and spends his money for love of Him, on the kindred and the orphans and the needy and the wayfarer and those who ask *for charity,* and for *ransoming* the captives; and who observes Prayer and pays the Zakāt; and those who fulfil their promise when they have made

---

[2] *Surah* 92, Verses 15-22
[3] *Surah* 76, Verses 9-10.
[4] *Surah* 3, Verses 134-135.

one, and the patient in poverty and afflictions and
the steadfast in time of war; it is these who have
proved truthful and it is these who are the God-
fearing. [5]

And help one another in righteousness
and piety; but help not one another in sin and
transgression. And fear Allah; surely, Allah is
severe in punishment. [6]

Islam stresses the value of good deeds, which are the consequences of human pity toward one's neighbour, just as it stresses
God's pity. The orphan, the poor, the humble, the unfortunate are
protected by the most concerned promptness. Islam declares that
brotherhood and charity are the two cornerstones of Muslim
society. This was a great achievement if we compare the Islamic
days with those of paganism, during which, as we see from
numerous passages of the Quran, the ruling class of plutocrats in
their pride and greediness despised and oppressed the poor; bad
faith was continually present in any sort of business transaction, and
no importance was given to the most elementary of duties toward
neighbours.

We shall cite only two of the many verses which deal with
justice:

. . . Judge between men with justice, and
follow not vain desire, lest it should lead thee astray
from the way of Allah. [7]

---

[5] *Surah* 2, Verse 178.

[6] *Surah* 5, Verse 3.

[7] *Surah* 38, Verse 27.

> Verily, Allah commands you to make over the trusts to those entitled to them, and when ye judge between men, you judge with justice. [8]

Everyone can judge for himself the deep sense of humanity inspired by the following passage from the Quran:

> Thy Lord has commanded, Worship none but Him, and *show* kindness to parents. If one of them or both of them attain old age with thee, never say unto them any word expressive of disgust nor reproach them, but address them with excellent speech.

> And lower to them the wing of humility out of tenderness. And say, 'My Lord, have mercy on them even as they nourished me in my childhood.' [9]

There are also some verses in the Quran which recall the evangelic teaching often referred to by the Christians as a burden of the morality of their religion:

> Repel evil with that which is best. [10]

We could continue with citations from the Quran, all of them of a very noble sort, but we think it may be valuable to mention a doctrine which is a more powerful inducement to the practice of virtue than any exhortation, namely the doctrine that this earthly life carries in it the seed of the future one: that any good deeds in this life will help one to reach supreme happiness in the next; that in order to approach the Almighty, purity of heart and honesty of

---

[8] *Surah* 4, Verse 59.
[9] *Surah* 17, Verses 24-25.
[10] *Surah* 23, Verse 97.

deeds is necessary; and that everyone will be presented, when in front of God, with the results of his efforts.

> Then whoso does an atom's weight of good
> will see it,
> And whoso does an atom's weight of evil
> will *also* see it. [11]

> Surely, Allah wrongs not *any one even* by the weight of an atom. And if there be a good deed, He multiplies it and gives from Himself a great reward. [12]

On the other hand, horrible and very painful punishments are reserved for the wicked and the evil-doers. The last judgment is presented in fiery colours. God, the supreme judge of the universe, will ask the good ones to leave the destroyed world and join Him in the heart of His mercy, while He will cast into the burning abyss of Gehenna all those who did not pay attention to the admonishments of the prophets.

It is necessary, here, to refute another accusation that is raised by the non-believers, that Islam has promised to its followers a sensual paradise with the gazelle-eyed houris, rivers of milk and honey, delicious fruits, luxurious vegetation and a graduated scale of highly material pleasures. Such accusations forget that it was not possible for the sons of the desert to understand promises of enjoyment of highly rarified spiritual prizes. For them, it was necessary to give a realistic description of paradise, almost a tangible one, in simple words. Only later on when they had reached higher spiritual levels would it have been possible to speak to the Bedouin in terms of worshipping God in humility and love. It is,

---

[11] *Surah* 99, Verses 8-9.
[12] *Surah* 4, Verse 41.

however, rank calumny to say that Muhammad and his followers took these realistic descriptions literally, since from the outset they found a deeper meaning in them than the description could show, namely that the greatest happiness would be, according to Al-Ghazali, in the beautified visions of the soul in the presence of the Almighty when the curtain which separates man from God is finally cast aside and the celestial glory appears in all its effulgence.

To support a similar conception of paradise, a tradition says, "The most favored by God will be those who will see the glory of God by day and night and will enjoy a happiness as far superior to all the pleasures of the body as the ocean is superior to a drop of sweat."

How then will the Almighty judge the deeds of His servants? Will that be done on the basis of some external standard, or according to their consequences? No. The Quran plainly states that God looks upon intention and motive, the *niyya,* with which deeds were accomplished, and this is the basis for a spiritual evaluation of deeds. It states that the strict observance of the law, if not accompanied by acts of mercy and charity, will have little value with God, and that an egotistical or hypocritical motivation will take away all value from a good deed. We have already seen the same concept when we were discussing formalities in the practices of the cult. Now we see it repeated again respecting the deeds of the believer. The cult has to be "pure". [13] And, it must proceed from the "soundness" and "righteousness" of heart. [14]

Hypocrisy and pride are so vigorously attacked in this religion that at certain points they are treated as a mild form of polytheism, for, according to some writers, men who act on these motives

---

[13] *Surah* 98, Verse 3.
[14] *Surah* 26, Verse 90 and *Surah* 22, Verse 33.

actually associate the idea of God with the desire of gaining consideration among other men.

Like other religions, Islam gives an explanation of an age-old problem that continues to puzzle the human mind, namely, why is it that the wicked appear to enjoy the favours of fortune while the good are often hit by great misfortunes. Islam teaches that God grants to rebels, tyrants and unjust ones, a waiting period which may even go as far as their death. But the moment will come in which He will reward and punish. It teaches that through misfortunes, God often tests His servants so as to make manifest the spirit of resignation with which they humbly submit themselves to His wishes, saying, "We belong to God and we shall return to Him."

The Muslim tradition brings to us a most beautiful definition of mercy and charity, coupled with a most delicate definition of moral concepts. It is well known that the lines of the Quran, which taken alone would not have been sufficient to regulate all human life in its various contingencies, have been continued, supplemented and brought to fulfillment by a mass of traditional sayings which go back to the Prophet. It matters little if in respect of some of these sayings the question of authenticity and of antiquity is raised. Even if we grant that they do not all go back to Muhammad himself, yet the majority embody the spirit of the ancient Muslim community which had blended together in itself the real spirit of Islam, and they bring to us the concepts and aspirations of that community. The reader may judge of the beauty and meaning of the following traditional sayings:

The one who caresses the head of an orphan
will receive in the day of resurrection an extra light
for each hair his hand touched.

To each house there is a key; the key to paradise is love for the little ones and the poor.

No one is a believer if he does not wish for his brother that which he wishes for himself.

But the most inclusive saying of all is that of the old vagabond who was converted to Islam:

The Prophet has given me a seven-fold exhortation: 1—love the poor and be close to them; 2—always look at those who are below you and never towards those who are above you; 3— never ask anything of anybody; 4—always be devoted to your parents, even if they annoy you; 5—always tell the truth even if it is bitter; 6—don't let insults take you away from the way of God; 7—often repeat— "there is no strength and power outside of God"— because this is a part of the treasure which is hidden under the throne of God.

When, later on, mysticism enters into Islam, a still higher ideal will be set before the human soul: that man's perfection and man's happiness rest in the effort to imitate God's qualities and to understand the real essence of His attributes. [15]

From the traditional sayings another doctrine arises which gives a distinctive reputation to Islam. God does not limit His mercy to man alone but looks upon animals too with love and tenderness. The lives of animals being for Him on the same basis as

---

[15] This again is based upon a saying of the Prophet:
  "Equip yourselves with the attributes of God."

that of a man, it follows that if man does not want to invoke divine anger he must have regard for animals; he must always see that they are given food and drink, and that they have the necessary sustenance and rest.

Islam, while through the Quran and the Sunna, shows man the road to virtue, does not forget the needs of human nature, any more than it ignored man's weaknesses when it established the practices of the cult. When Islam gives man a moral perspective to which he can turn in desperation, it does not go beyond the limits of reality, nor does it present an ideal of virtue which would be unreachable save by the few elect. Instead it establishes healthy principles of life which prove in their application to be of a genuine and admirable practicability. By presenting a model of integrity and honesty, it does not depart from the law of life, but remains close to human nature and takes into consideration the just aspiration of an honest happiness. Far from creating a difference between the religious life of the individual and his behavior in the world, it looks towards the creation of a society where man is at the same time a member of it and also a devoted servant of God.

According to the Muslims, the best way for man to express his thanks to God is to make good use of that which God has bestowed upon him. To take advantage of the good things which God has put at the disposal of everybody, is not only a possibility but, we shall say, a duty, if there is in these good things nothing which could be dangerous to the individual himself or to his neighbour. The Quran says:

> On those who believe and do good works
> there shall be no sin for what they eat, provided they
> fear *God* and believe and do good works, and again

fear *God* and believe, yet again fear *God* and do good. And Allah loves those who do good. [16]

Say, 'Who has forbidden the adornment of Allah which He has produced for His servants, and the good things of *His* providing?' [17]

Tradition is the strongest support for a healthy conception of life. Here we repeat what we have said already when we spoke of traditions which contain the highest moral concepts. What does it matter if somebody does raise the question of authenticity? The Muslim world accepts these traditional sayings today as true and for the most part follow their instructions.

A famous tradition says, "There is no monasticism in Islam." [18] As a matter of fact Islam does not care for asceticism with its useless mortification of the flesh, its unnecessary deprivations as well as its continuous fasts and nights spent in prayer. In regard to marriage, the Islamic tradition asks for no more than an honest and constructive life in which the individual follows the middle of the road, remembering God on the one side and respecting, on the other, the rights and needs of the body, family, and society.

The Prophet said.

The best among you is not the one who forgets the life after death in order to enjoy the present,

---

[16] *Surah* 5, Verse 94.

[17] *Surah* 7, Verse 33.

[18] This is laid down in the Quran in the following verse:

Then We caused Our Messengers to follow in their footsteps; and We caused Jesus, son of Mary, to follow *them,* and We gave him the Gospel. And We placed in the hearts of those who accepted him compassion and mercy. But monasticism which they invented for themselves—We did not prescribe it for them. *(Surah* 57, Verse 28).

nor the one who does the contrary; the best among
you is the one who takes from both.

To a too fervent youngster he said:
Your body has its rights and your wife has
her rights and your guest has his rights.

To the one who one day asked his advice about alms, he said:
Give one-third because one-third is already
enough. It is better to leave your descendants
provided for than to compel them to go begging.

Strict celibacy is the subject of severe criticism in Islam and it
is against the customs established by Muhammad. To an Arab who
was following such a celibate life, Muhammad, according to
tradition, spoke this very bitter reproach, "Have you decided to
become a son of Satan? Do you want to be like a Christian monk?
If you do, then stand forth openly and associate yourself with them.
Or are you one of our men? If so, then you have to follow our way.
Our way is the married life."

The limitations upon the enjoyment of life which Islam has
imposed on its followers are but few, are equal for all, and show
great wisdom. Today when a severe battle is being fought in the
Western world against alcoholism and when the West tries to limit
gambling by means of prohibitions and limitations, can anybody
blame Islam for having banged shut these two "doors of danger",
these causes of corruption both of the spirit and of wealth? Thrift is
a virtue in the words of the Quran, but this is not enough. We read
in the holy book of prohibition of gambling and of making money
through charging interest on loans. Would you not say that God's
wisdom shines in this repression of illegal earnings?

Men feel the need of a religion, but at the same time they want it to answer their needs and they want it to be not only close to their sentiments but to offer tranquility and security for the other life as well as for this. Islam answers these prerequisites perfectly, for it is not only a creed but also a philosophy of life. It teaches right-thinking, proper acting, and honest speaking, and for these reasons it finds its way to both the mind and the heart of man without difficulty.

CHAPTER V

Islamic Rule and Civilization

We must offer our deepest admiration to a religion which does not stop with a theory suited to the aspirations of human nature, nor with establishing a code of the highest rules which man can live by, but which goes on to inculcate a philosophy of life; which puts the basic principles of morality on a systematic and positive basis; which translates the duty of man towards himself and others into precise rules, which are capable of evolution and are compatible with the highest intellectual development; and, to crown it all, which provides a sanction for these laws. The influence of such a religion upon the lives of men generally, but more particularly upon those of the ignorant and the uneducated, is both continuous and healthy, since for them moral precepts have little value unless they are enunciated with the precision of a law and carry with them well-defined penalties.

Islam is such a religion. Once human nature's essential need of being guided more by authority than by sermons and abstract principles was recognized, Islam spoke to it in terms of a positive command from an absolute power. This was another cause of its great success. If Islam succeeded in creating a united and strong nation based on moral principles in an Arabia where the most complete anarchy then reigned, where the idea of government as an independent social institution was completely unknown, where any form of human authority was considered unbearable, where cruelty was the rule, and where killing and stealing were not punishable crimes but only acts which invited reprisals by the family or tribe of the dead or injured person, this could only be achieved because Islam was both a law and a religion.

The *Sharia,* the canon law of Islam, is not confined to ritual. All aspects of public and private life are subject to its rulings and it has the purpose of relating every act of the individual with his religious duties. All branches of the law are represented in it.

The law makers in passing laws with their various moral implications could not always go back to the Quran, since only a very few verses of judicial character are to be found there, and even these speak in very broad terms. Nor could they go to the Sunna which, although an ample complement to the Book, is yet quite inadequate to solve the numerous cases to which everyday life gives rise. As a result, we witness in the Muslim world the establishment of the principle of the Ijma or the consensus of the opinions of the Muslims—to be more specific, of the Muslims who were recognized as being the most educated at any given time. This consensus of the best opinions is recognized as having binding authority.

The Prophet said, "My community will never unite on error." These points which this group will unanimously recognize as correct and just ought to be accepted as true and just, and the laws established on the basis of such an agreement have a compulsory character.

Ijma, which has been the keystone of the historic evolution of Islam, will also be the evolutionary power of its development.

It allowed laws existing among peoples of other than Arabic origin, if not in conflict with the law of God, to become part of Islamic law. It will once again be by means of this factor that Islam, if it will cast off that kind of stiffness into which the Muslim world seems to have fallen recently (and promising signs are already seen on the horizon), will move freely again and adapt itself to the needs of modern times.

Thanks to Ijma, the Islamic law has accepted, incorporated and completed laws which were in existence long before the mission of Muhammad. But since their value is not in question, we shall not pause here to discuss them, nor shall we discuss those articles of the Islamic law whose wisdom is taken for granted. We shall turn instead to see what defence can be offered of those Islamic social institutions which are especially under criticism and attack by the non-believers.

The Quran, as we have already mentioned, has established very few rules in such a precise fashion as to constitute law. In the majority of cases, it has left to the discretion of its followers the freedom of conforming to those institutions which would be appropriate to the time and to the country in which they live. Wonderful sign of God's mercy! Definite rules have, however, been established on marriage, stating that nobody may marry women with whom there is a certain degree of blood-relationship. To this no objection is raised by the non-Muslim. The argument begins, however, and rages very powerfully when we come to the question of polygamy, which, under certain conditions which we shall discuss later on, has been permitted by the Quran.

We could begin by stating that it has not yet been proved in any absolute way that polygamy is necessarily a social evil, an obstacle on the road to progress, but we prefer not to discuss the matter on this plane. We could also make the point that in certain stages of social development, when certain particular conditions exist—an unusually high number of males killed in war, for instance—polygamy becomes a social necessity. At any rate, it should not be judged by the concepts of later ages, because in Muhammad's day it was fully accepted and legally recognized not only among the Arabs but also among other peoples of that region. As a matter of fact, the Islamic law, which seems today to be so full of concessions on this subject, actually established for the followers of Muhammad certain limitations upon polygamy which was in practice without any limitation. It condemned certain forms of conditional and temporary marriage which were in effect different forms of legal concubinage. Furthermore, it gave to the woman rights she had never known before. All this could easily be established and documented were it not even more important to present to the reader another aspect of the question.

The Quran has allowed a man to marry two, three and even four women. But, at the same time, it has specified a qualifying condition which is indispensable for such marriages by insisting upon the husband exercising the most perfect and complete justice towards each wife, meaning by "justice" not only equal treatment in material provisions but also equal love: ". . marry but two, or three, or four; and if you fear that you will not deal justly, then *marry only one*." [1]

In the same chapter where this rule is laid down, some other verses make it clear that such a spirit of equality due to human nature is rare indeed to find in man:

> And you cannot keep *perfect* balance between wives, however much you may desire it. [2]

---

[1] *Surah* 4, Verse 4.
[2] *Surah* 4, Verse 130.

Reasoning from the above we conclude that polygamy, although proved possible, is practically made impossible by the difficulty of fulfilling the condition which is its prerequisite. God's rule is indeed a prohibition, say both Ez Zahrawi and Ameer Ali. We cannot argue on behalf of polygamy by merely stating that it is acceptable to God, nor can we take as evidence the personal life of the Prophet, which was the result of his personal condition of exceptional responsibilities. Too many differences exist between him and other men in the fulfillment of the condition of justice, as well as in respect of the problems and difficulties with which he was faced.

Enemies of Islam have insisted in depicting Muhammad as a sensual individual and a dissolute man, trying to find in his marriages evidence of a weak character not consistent with his mission. They refuse to take into consideration the fact that during those years of his life when by nature the sexual urge is strongest, although he lived in a society like that of the Arabs, where the institution of marriage was almost non-existent, where polygamy was the rule, and where divorce was very easy indeed, he was married to one woman alone, Khadija, who was much older than himself, and that for twenty-five years he was her faithful, loving husband. Only when she died and when he was already fifty years old did he marry again and more than once. Each of these marriages had a social or a political reason, for he wanted through the women he married to honour pious women, or to establish marriage relations with other clans and tribes for the purpose of opening the way for the propagation of Islam. With the sole exception of Ayesha, he married women who were neither virgins. nor young nor beautiful. Was this sensuality?

He was man and not God, and the desire of a son may also have brought him to other marriages, for unforunately the ones born to Khadija had died. Without too many resources, he took upon his shoulders the heavy burden of maintaining a large family, but always, in spite of the number of his wives, he observed a perfect equality towards all of them, nor did he ever use in respect of any one of them the right of separation. He acted under the sanction of reversed ancient patriarchs like Moses and others, to whose plural marriages, nobody seems to take exception. Could this be because we do not have the particulars of their daily lives, while in the case of Muhammad we know all about his life within the family? Unfortunately, men in the past, not listening to the critical second half of the Quranic verse which invites people to monogamy, have paid attention only to the first part of it, the one which allows them to be polygamists, and have taken advantage of the concessions granted to them, without interpreting, as was necessary the word of God. Today in the Islamic world, particularly in those countries which have seen a new flourishing of civilization, new moral sentiments are gaining ground, and the practice of polygamy, thanks to various circumstances, has become very restricted.

The Quran permits divorce. Since Western society has also accepted divorce and in fact has recognized it as a necessity of life and almost everywhere has given to it full legal sanction, we could omit any defence of its recognition by Islam. Yet by discussing it and comparing the habits of the pre-Islamic Arab society and the Muslim law, we will have the opportunity of showing that the law of Islam in this respect also inaugurated a social reform.

Prior to the time of Muhammad, divorce had been made very easy by current practice among the Arabs. It was enough for the man to say one word alone, to make a single sign, to send his wife back to her family. It was also enough for the wife (even if this practice was not too common, nevertheless examples are not lacking in pre-Islamic society) to turn the entrance flap of the tent inside out to signify that she had broken the marriage tie. Now the law of God lays down certain rules which not only permit but in certain circumstances recommend the cancellation of the divorce. The husband, after having pronounced the words of separation, reserves for a certain period of time, during which the wife lives by herself and cannot marry again, the right to take her back without any formality. It is only at the end of that period of retirement or if the formality of separation has been pronounced under special conditions, that the separation becomes definite. The woman has no right to ask for a divorce, but she may ask for cancellation of her marriage by applying to the judge, and this if she has a good reason. The purpose of this limitation on the woman's initiative is to put a check on the practice of divorce, for men are supposed to be less susceptible to decisions on the spur of the moment than women are. The intervention of the judge is also designed to secure to the woman all her financial and other rights in working out the dissolution of the marriage.

This rule, and the other one, which lays down that in case of disagreement within the family conciliators have to be consulted in order to promote an agreement, would by itself be evidence that Islam considers divorce as reprehensible. The following verses of the Quran state this in a very positive way:

> For those who vow *abstinence* from their wives, the maximum period of waiting is four months; then if they go back from the vow, surely, Allah is Most Forgiving, Merciful.

> And if they decide upon divorce, then surely, Allah is All-Hearing, All-Knowing. [3]

Several traditions carry the same idea, for instance:

> God hasn't created anything which he loves more than the emancipation of man, nothing which he hates more than divorce.

---

[3] *Surah* 2, Verses 227-228.

In order to avoid incitement towards misconduct and prevent its consequences, the Muslim woman must carry a veil, and cover all of her body, leaving uncovered only those parts of her body such as eyes and feet, the freedom of which is absolutely necessary. This is done not out of any lack of esteem towards women, nor to suppress their will, but to protect them from the desire of men. This centuries-old rule of the secluded life for women and the resulting moral life had the effect in oriental countries of making commercialized prostitution entirely unknown, except where foreigners' influence was exercised. As no one can deny the value of such gains we must conclude that the custom of the veil and that of the non-participation of women in public life, while from a certain point of view they represent a loss, from another point of view have been sources of incalculable benefit to Muslim society.

In those countries where education, the necessary prerequisite to women's freedom, is not shared by all, there is much to be said for women's abstention from public life in spite of modern ideologies and the spread of western influence. This does not mean that conditions will continue in the rigid form which they assume at present in most of the countries of the East. Such a concept would be contrary to the very spirit of Islam, which is one of continuous adaptation to the contingencies of different times and peoples.

> O Prophet? tell thy wives and thy daughters and the women of the believers that they should draw close to them portions of their *loose* outer coverings. That is nearer that they may *thus* be distinguished and not molested. And Allah is Most Forgiving, Merciful.[4]

> And say to the believing women that they restrain their eyes and guard their private parts, and

---

[4] *Surah* 33, Verse 60.

that they disclose not their *natural and artificial* beauty except that which is apparent thereof, and that they draw their head-coverings over their bosoms. [5]

These words of the Quran have to be understood with the just moderation which is found in the habits of the Prophet who left to the women of his family a considerable freedom. If this is not understood, we could not explain the part which many of the women took in the political and war-like events of the time during the life and after the death of Muhammad, such as the role of Ayesha in the fighting against Ali (during the battle known as the battle of the camel, she urged the soldiers and was exposed to serious danger), or the role of Fatima Bint Qays al Fihriyyah in the circumstances leading to the election of Caliph Othman, or many other events of primitive Islam.

But if, from the social point of view in Europe, woman has reached a high condition, her position, legally at least, until a very few years ago, has been and in some countries continues to be, less independent than that of the Muslim woman in the Islamic world. The Muslim woman, besides having the right to inherit together with her brothers, even if in a smaller proportion, of not being given in marriage without her free consent, and of not being mistreated by her husband, also possesses the right of receiving a dowry from the husband, of being supported by him, even if she is wealthy by birth, and of enjoying the most complete freedom, if she is legally capable, in the administration of her personal estate.

The institution of slavery which began, we may say, with the establishment of human society and which has lasted through the ages and among all peoples right up to our own day, was not

---

[5] *Surah* 24, Verse 32.

altogether abolished by divine law, and the non-Muslims have made a major accusation of this fact.

First of all, the condition of slaves among the Muslims, whether the Muslims are nomads or settled on land, is far more tolerable than the Europeans like to believe (testimonials of this can be found in the word of many a European who visits oriental countries), and it is unfair to compare slavery in the East with that existing, for instance, a century ago in the United States of America. What humane feeling is there in the tradition, "Don't call him 'my slave' but 'my youth'; and don't call your slave girl 'maid', but 'my daughter'." If we are to consider these facts from an historical point of view, we shall see, even in this field, the wonderful work of reform done by the Prophet of God. Not only did he restrict slavery (While in the pre-Islamic time it was possible for a free man to lose his freedom for failure to pay his debts, no Muslim could make a slave of another Muslim.) but rules, both positive and negative were introduced, and appeals were made to the believers to go forward and, in due time bring about a gradual emancipation of all slaves. Certainly, under the beneficial influence of these admonitions of freeing of the slaves would have been achieved if slavery had not had such strong tenacious roots in the habits, not only of the Arab people, but in those of all nations towards conquered or nearly conquered peoples. Emancipation has also been prevented by men under the urge of their perversity, having wrongly interpreted God's word as an authorization to keep slavery alive.

In the Quran it is said several times that the freeing of slaves is the penalty for certain sins. [6] And in traditions it is strongly affirmed

---

[6] See *Surah* 4, Verse *93; Surah* 5, Verse 90; *Surah* 24, Verse 34; *Surah* 58, Verse 4; *Surah* 90, Verse 14.

that freeing a slave is a deed most acceptable to God. "The one who frees a slave who believes, shall in the day of resurrection, be freed from Hell."

Guided by the spirit of the Quran and by traditions, several schools of Islamic law established rules which made compulsory or vigorously promoted the emancipation of slaves. We cannot list all of these here. We shall only mention two of them which prove how a slave could, by his own efforts, according to the Muslim law, raise himself to the condition of a free man, if the owner could not or would not bear the financial loss which would result from the emancipation. He could obtain from his master a legal document binding himself, immediately after becoming a free man, to pay as soon as possible the agreed compensation to his former master. Or, he could ask his master to let him earn by his work (and such a concession is a very worthy one), the necessary amount to pay for his freedom. The Quran says:

> And (those of your slaves) who desire a *deed of manumission* in writing, execute it for them.[7]

There is also another point. The Muslim state took upon itself the obligation of helping, with funds coming from legal alms, those slaves who needed help in purchasing their freedom!

Islam, which has never made any distinction of race or colour among men, which considered the white and the black, the nomad and the settled farmer, the ruler and the subject as all alike, not only in theory but also in practice (and as a matter of fact in the tent, in the palace, in the mosque, in the market, they all mingled together without reserve and with no sign of contempt or arrogance towards each other), never countenanced any humiliating treatment for

---

[7] *Surah* 24, Verse 34.

slaves. Is it not fitting to remember here, while talking of the social equality imposed by Islam, the beautiful episode of King Jabale, who, having become a Muslim, went in great state to Mecca. While he was making the ritual tour around the Ka'ba, he struck a Bedouin who had accidentally trodden on his rich mantle. The Caliph Omar ruled that he was to receive a similar blow from the Bedouin because in Islam all men are alike. Jabale refused to submit to this and that very night he left with his five hundred knights and went straight to Byzantium where he became a Christian. Many years later, in the midst of honours and riches, the memories of Islam still filled his eyes with tears.

History furnishes many examples of slaves to whom high and honourable positions were given (among others, Bilal, who because of his beautiful voice was accorded the high honour of being the first muezzin in Islam) and of freedmen who occupied high government positions, even rising to the Caliphate. Here, before we pass on to another topic, it would be appropriate to remember that Muhammad strictly forbade all mutilations of slaves, and that the custom of having the women's quarters guarded by eunuchs began only at the time of the Omayyad Caliphs.

In connection with the penal law, it is known that the law of God did not institute a new penal system. This is because in Muhammad's time it was not possible to make great modifications in this field, and also because it is in the spirit of Islam to leave the most complete freedom to people in establishing laws which are suited to their nature and their time. Nevertheless, Islam brought some improvement in regard to the old law, principally eliminating the most dangerous consequences of the right of retribution. It established, in full agreement with progressive laws and civilization, the principle that the guilty one must be found and punished, but only in a few cases are any precise rules either suggested or established. What Muhammad actually did was to reconfirm punishments already existing prior to Islam in the laws of countries, such as retaliation, mutilation, and lynching. "And there is life for you in *the law of* retaliation," says the Quran. [8] The fear of punishment as heavy as the crime itself, it was believed, would arrest the hand of the man about to commit a crime. If you consider, from the point of view of crime prevention, the very stiff penalties for homicide, injuries, lust, calumny, drunkenness, theft and robbery, you will feel that they are very wise, particularly if they are coupled with the very frequent Quranic exaltation of pardon as something agreeable to the Lord, and of moderation in asking the price of blood or the payment of liabilities. They also have to be examined in the light of a fundamental principle in Islamic law, that for disobedience to God, the believer must do everything possible to avoid inflicting punishment on the sinner; God having based His relationship with men on pity and kindness. Finally, they must be regarded in the light of the many requirements which in practice make very difficult a literal application of all the penalties established by the Quran.

---

[8] *Surah* 2, Verse 180.

CHAPTER VI

The Significance of Mysticism in Islam

As time went on, Islam, like other religions, developed a mystic and contemplative element, either resulting from a natural inner evolution or from external influences. At the outset, in Islam, when the observance of the duties of daily life was placed above religions speculation, this mystical element had no possibility of developing. The desire of making a direct and immediate approach to the Creator, of being in contact with Him was the essential basis of all real devotion. The need, therefore, of an intuitive knowledge of God is part of faith.

Born from this need of the believer, Islamic mysticism, or as it is called in technical terminology, Sufism, found its first element in the deep sentiment of communion with God which the Prophet so often enjoyed when he spoke to his followers, and in the example of his deep mercy. It also found in the widespread diffusion of neo-Platonic theories, a sympathetic field for its evolution. But let us be precise about this. The idea that the verses of the Quran contained a deep and hidden meaning over and above the one which first appeared from the reading, did not develop out of any desire of escaping the strictness of the text and of the dogmas, but rather from the conviction that the words of the divine book meant more and not less than what the common interpretation had seen in them.

In the oldest statements pertaining to the concepts of the inner light, there is no support for the theory that the Prophet or the direct heirs of his spiritual teaching invited men to give up responsible life in the world in order to cultivate faith and achieve the inner fulfillment of religious practices. Asceticism and all its manifestations, as we have already said, were denounced by the Prophet. Nevertheless, in their longing to reach spiritual perfection, many Muslims forgot that human existence must be a continuous struggle, and from early times, either as a reaction to the almost pagan excess of liberties evolved during the time of the Omayyads, or as a reaction of disgust at the political events which were against their pious feelings, or for other causes, these protesters separated themselves from the world and moved into a kind of life entirely dedicated to the worshipping of God.

From piety to quietism, the step is short. From quietism to mysticism, the evolution is natural. The ancient communion with God, the intuitive feeling that the Almighty was unreachable in the midst of the distractions of a mundane life, resulted in a theory of spiritual development basing itself in Islam, as in other religions, on the complete abnegation of the individual and upon his absolute dedication to a contemplative life. Man, finding himself and freeing himself of material things, must make every effort to react to God's beauty and goodness. He must detach himself from the externals of his personal life, in order to succeed in uniting his spirit with the divine existence, the only reality. This was a very high purpose, one which could not fail to attract souls in search of a high degree of spirituality. It did much good to the Muslims, because while it impressed on them the idea of the possibility of a spiritual union with God through long and laborious training, it developed the feeling of spiritual dignity, and in place of a blind and meticulous obedience it established self-education through ascetic discipline and saved the soul from capitulating to a materialistic standard.

Unfortunately Sufism, once it was removed from any form of discipline, soon shaped itself in the minds of many Muslims in forms quite contrary to the fundamental concepts preached by Muhammad. As a result, pantheistic ideas, new and strange codes, and corrupt moral concepts began to emerge. A grave danger threatened Islam. On the other hand, a danger which we cannot be sure, may not be even graver than these forms of degeneration within mysticism was developing, to wit, the rise of dogmatic theology (unfortunately, the desire of imposing conformity and of repressing heresy has always been the curse of all religious systems), made barren by empty discussion of extremely subtle questions which the mass of people could not understand, except in terms of the conduct of life. This dogmatic theology ended by freezing itself into a type of very hard formalism which could no longer satisfy the religious aspirations of the human soul. What is even more tragic, the majority of doctors, instead of occupying themselves with theological questions, dedicated their time to the study, considered by them to be of paramount importance, of the divine law in its various practical applications. But, having lost sight of broad and healthy conceptions, they lost themselves in miserable discussions of the most fantastic and detailed casuistry.

For Islam's sake, in this difficult period of its life, a great genius, a great renovator, Al-Ghazali came to the rescue of this depressed and abused religion, giving it a new, healthy, fresh and powerful vitality. His invitation to a mystical life based on the preservation of the orthodox principles, and remembering the examples set by the companions of the Prophet, gave a new beauty to Islam and revived its earlier vitality. He claimed that the development of the religious life understood as the Sufis did, must be founded on the practical precepts of Islam, while "the door" which would admit us into it would be a knowledge of the law, which must always be the starting point of the mystical ascent and of intuitive knowledge *of* God. The ideas of AI-Ghazali as accepted by the *Ijma* became the corner-stone on which Islam founded the final construction of its ideas and its religious aspects, ridding itself of the degeneration into which it had been led by the unrestrained impetuousness of the most extreme mystics. Religion saw its horizon broadened, and returned to purity and continuity of thought and sentiment, and it became an experience of deep inner origin in which love for God was the central point. In this way it influenced the life of the Muslims in the most noble and intimate fashion.

The intensive part of the mystical philosophy established itself in the monasteries of the various brotherhoods. The Zavies, Ribats, and the Khankahs sprang up in many parts of the Muslim world. Wherever a saint, a marabout, Wali, Pir or Sidi, or whatever the different countries chose to name him, made his home and raised his voice and told of his direct visions of God, disciples grouped around him, and here religious orders were founded and mystic teaching was given.

But as only very few men can be truly called saints, we always find closely associated with the sincere and honest ones a large number of pseudo-saints, the cheaters who trade on the gullibility of the people, as well as a certain collection of the ignorant and the fools, whose minds have been upset by mystical practices. While the teaching of the real saints is beneficial, the influence of the pseudo-saints is very deplorable. But how are we to recognize the good and true ones? The quietism of the Sufi was also a danger for the social life, because, in its extreme manifestations, it generated a spirit of passive reliance on God and in His Providence and thus encouraged an unwillingness on the part of the devout person to provide for his daily needs himself. Therefore, without doubt, there must be charged to Sufism a partial responsibility for the present-day decline of the Muslim nations. But, on the other hand, can we deny the great benefit which came to Islam from the work of these brotherhoods? These sources of religious life kept the spirit alive throughout all the Muslim lands right out to the extreme boundaries and were like so many oases scattered in the vastness of the desert.

It is, however, unfair on the part of non-Muslims to judge the very essence of the Islamic religion by certain external regulations of mystical codes. For these are regarded quite as critically by most educated and intelligent Muslims.

Mohammad Ferid Wagdi writes:

> Europeans must be forgiven if they believe all calumnies against Islam and against the Muslims and they are right if they show hostility toward our religion, as long as they have in front of their eyes nothing else than showings of "novelties" created by men of poor judgment, accepted and increased by the population with other forms which are suspected of heresies and errors and which are contrary to human nature and the laws of civilization. How can we hope that Europeans will understand the very essence of our religion, which is the only one which will carry all happiness, as long as they only know certain external features of Islam which they witness every day like the noisy crowds in streets going after flags and drums; the very objectionable ceremonies that are contrary to all moral reasonings which take place in all the cities of Egypt upon the birthday of the Prophet; the reunions in large circles in front of a public of thousands of people; the mystic litany yelled in a powerful voice with the accompaniment of bowing to the right and left; and similar things?
>
> The learned oriental has two duties: first to make known to all the world that the Islamic religion, besides being free from many of the errors

which writers generally attribute to it, and from that form of cult which the mass wants to give it, in the presence of spectators, is in reality the code of true happiness, that it is the angel of real civilization and consequently that everybody owes respect and love to it, like that given it by the great philosophers who started it and believed in it; the second duty which rests with the educated Muslim is to make an effort to do away with the heresies which drag down the Islamic world and represent a dark spot on the Orient, a cause of derision for everyone who has a scrap of judgment.

CHAPTER VII

Islam and its Relation to Science

Rational speculation is, as Muhammad Abduh states, the foundation of Islam. As we have seen, in order to awaken in man faith in One God, it does not use miracles, but the ordinary faculty of human reason. Later on, when, in order to awaken belief in the Prophets and in the divine revelations, Islam presents that great miracle known as the Quran (which is in itself both an understandable science and the intelligible word of God) it does not expect that man should accept Islam with passive faith, without the active application of his intelligence. Rather, it invites him to understand it to meditate upon it up to the limit which human intelligence and reason permit, and it challenges him to find a way to deny its superiority by finding a work which could be its equal. [1]

The importance which is assigned to reason in Islam is such that for the majority of Muslims (I refer here always to the thought of Muhammad Abduh) when there is an irreconcilable conflict between an alleged tradition and reason, the latter must prevail and

---

[1] *Surah* 2, Verse 24.

the tradition must be rejected as spurious. As a matter of fact, there are only two paths to follow: either we admit that the way tradition dictates is unintelligible, or we must interpret it in consonance with reason. For believers to accept all the mass of tradition just as it is, some of it verging upon absurdity, is not expected or required in Islam.

Now a religion which has as its basis rational speculation, and which gives such a broad scope to reason, a religion that orders the use of all the faculties bestowed upon man by God and consequently also the one which is the greatest of all, namely, his intelligence—how could such a religion be an obstacle in the way of science and philosophy?

It has been said that modern civilization has achieved such a happy development in Europe because Christianity has separated the civil power from the religious one, as well as because the present-day Western states are free from Church influence, which through centuries was exercised on them, while in Islamic countries such separation cannot be effected because the civil power is connected by law with the religious one.

Now Islam is in the fullest sense a religion and a state. In addition to having revealed God to man, it also establishes rights and duties and recognizes that authority is needed to have these observed. But the Caliph is not, for the Muslim, a religious head. He is not infallible. He does not claim God's inspiration and does not pretend to be able to explain the Quran and the tradition as a binding authority. In order to administer justice, he must be able to understand enough of the Sources so that he will be able to see the difference between truth and falsehood, but he is like all other Muslims in his understanding of the sacred book. He will be obeyed as long as he keeps within the proper limits.

If he should overstep them, his subjects would have the right to call him back to his duty, to admonish him, and, if he should not pay attention to their word, to elect a new Caliph in his place. A famous tradition says, "In the case of rebellion towards the Creator, no obedience is due by man."

The Caliph is, consequently, from all points of view, a civilian arbitrator and is not a theocrat who receives his power from God and who has the right to be obeyed by his subjects as a necessary consequence of their belief. In Islam there is only one religious power, if we can so designate a power which consists in the strength granted by God to all Muslims, from the humblest to the noblest, of encouraging the believers to follow the good road and to keep away from evil. The quadi, the mufti, the shaikh-ul-Islam have only civil power, because none of them could impose his authority contrary to the faith of one of his brothers.

How can we say that Islam hampered the development of culture in the past centuries, when the courts and schools of Islam were lighthouses of culture for a Europe which was at that time in the midst of the darkness of the Middle Ages; when the thoughts of Arab philosophers reached such heights that they led the way for Western scholars; when Harun-er-Rashid required a school for the study of various sciences to be attached to each mosque; and when libraries rich in hundreds of thousands of books were opened to scholars all over the Islamic world? Were not the Arabs the first who applied experimental methods, long before Bacon proclaimed their necessity? The development of chemistry, of astronomy, the propagation of Greek science, the promotion of the study of medicine and the discovery of various physical laws—are not these to the credit of the Arabs?

If this is so, then we cannot say that it is in the nature of their religion to create obstacles in the way of the progress of science. Let us say instead that at times statesmanship was compelled, in order to preserve peace in certain territories, to repress currents of thought which could become dangerous to the public order, that political and sometimes personal struggles, rather than religious causes, have in the past determined the attitudes of theologians, lawmakers, traditionists and philosophers. We must, however, recognize that today in certain Muslim environments there are strong objections to rational science and to modern industry. Afghans, Persians and Indians remain strongly bound to their old traditions. The people from the Maghrib are filled with exaggerated fanaticisms. There are still jurists who are so attached to the literal expressions of those books which they regard as fundamental that they refuse to express an opinion when a new case appears for which no clue is to be found in these old books. Or they try to keep the case in abeyance until they succeed in agreeing on a well-accepted opinion of one of their preferred authors. But it is not fair to accuse the spirit of Islam of rigidity and immobility, simply because of certain local situations that are to be found in particular historical conditions today or because of the over-rigid mentality of certain Muslim groups.

Unfortunately the Islamic religion, after having been an Arab treasure and having Arabized Greek science, fell into the hands of Turks, Tartan, and Mongols. These after having been employed by the Arabs as mercenaries and having come only to make money, took over the Islamic world, adopted the religion of the conquered, clothing themselves in its mantle without understanding its inner spirit or having their hearts educated by it. This incapacitated them from ever really entering into the genius of Islam. These barbarians are responsible for having tried to put to sleep the minds of their subjects, for making them lose their interest in science so that they could more easily be dominated. The new powers assumed for themselves, and themselves alone, the duty of deciding all affairs of the Muslim community, using the concept of divine predestination as a means of forbidding their subjects from thinking and for the purpose of establishing themselves on a solid basis for defending the idea that henceforth the doors of God's favours were closed to all newcomers. (How could that be as in the Quran, God reproaches this very sin in the followers of other religions.) [2]

In this way the faithful were forbidden to judge and forced to follow the opinions of their predecessors. It is these interlopers who, in a word, falsified the character of the religion they had embraced and followed its outer practices without understanding or being willing to understand its deeper spirit. This is how we account for the building up of that "rigidity" in Islam which has had such dangerous consequences, not only in religion or in law or in traditional literary and philosophical studies, but also in various manifestations of social life.

We do not believe it necessary to document this with further evidence. Fortunately this rigidity is a disease bound to disappear; as a matter of fact it already appears to be passing away. It is to the holy book which has never been altered at the hands either of its friends or its enemies, by either the learned or the unlettered, the book that time does not wear out but which remains just as it was revealed by God to the rough and simple Apostle, the last of all law-bearing Prophets—it is to this pure source that Muslims will return. As they drink directly from this holy book, they will not fail to be re-invigorated. There is strong evidence that this process has already begun.

---

[2] *Surah* 2, Verse 166.